Your Extraordinary Life
Choosing God's Best for Your Life

G. Allen Jackson

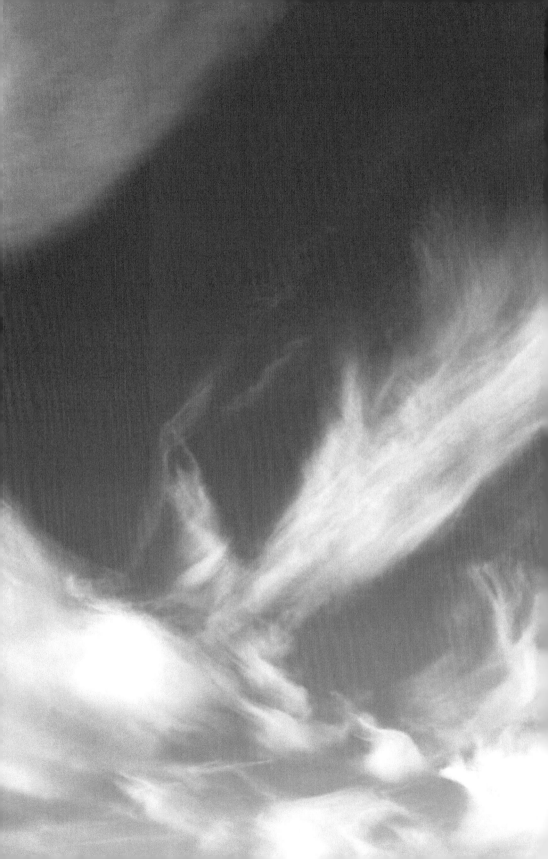

Contents

WELCOME

Has it ever occurred to you that one way to describe that "someplace" you are always trying to get to and that "something" you are always trying to find is to call it an extraordinary life. People call it a lot of other names (even simple living), but the best way I've found to describe the best God has planned for us is the extraordinary life.

Think of it this way: the ordinary life is the life anyone could lead; the extraordinary life is the only life you can lead. Because there's no one else like you, someone might be able to imitate you; but only you have the opportunity to live the life you were designed to live. The extraordinary life is what we're aiming for in this study. Not more churched or more religious people, but people who have decided between themselves and God not to settle for anything less than all He has for them.

Is the extraordinary life easy? Is it safe? Is it pain-free? If that's all you're looking for, you aren't looking for an extraordinary life, and whatever you do find won't satisfy, either!

We're going to meet some ordinary people in this study who are well on their way to living extraordinary lives. They are far from the stereotypical, cookie cutter Christians that so often get put before us as examples. These come with rough edges and real stories. They are following hard after God and their journey has been unique as only God could have planned it. Enjoy getting to know them a little better.

I trust you will discover the extraordinary life God has in mind for you. And I trust that in the company of others who are on the journey you will take some definite steps in becoming even more the person God designed you to be with the extraordinary life God intended for you to live.

G. Allen Jackson

USING THIS WORKBOOK

(Tools to Help You Have a Great Small Group Experience!)

1. Notice in the Table of Contents there are three sections:

(1) Sessions; (2) Appendix; and (3) Small Group Leaders. Familiarize yourself with the Appendix parts. Some of them will be used in the sessions themselves.

2. If you are facilitating/leading or co-leading a small group, the section Small Group Leaders will give you some hard-learned experiences of others that will encourage you and help you avoid many common obstacles to effective small group leadership.

3. Use this workbook as a guide, not a straightjacket. If the group responds to the lesson in an unexpected but honest way, go with that. If you think of a better question than the next one in the lesson, ask it. Take to heart the insights included in the Frequently Asked Questions pages and the Small Group Leaders section.

4. Enjoy your small group experience.

5. Read the Outline for Each Session on the next pages so that you understand how the sessions will flow.

Outline of Each Session

Most people want to live an extraordinary life, but few achieve this by themselves. And most small groups struggle to balance all of God's purposes in their meetings. Groups tend to overemphasize one of the various reasons for meeting. Rarely is there a healthy balance that includes teaching, evangelism, ministry, practical exercises, and worship. That's why we've included all of these elements in this study so you can live a healthy, balanced spiritual life over time.

A typical group session for *Your Extraordinary Life* will include the following:

Story.

The lessons we will learn during *Your Extraordinary Life* are best illustrated in the lives of real people. Each session will begin with a summary of someone's story and the video presentation during the session will capture firsthand that person telling their story.

Coming Together.

The foundation for spiritual growth is an intimate connection with God and his family. A few people who really know you and who earn your trust provide a place to experience the life Jesus invites you to live. This section of each session typically offers you two options. You can get to know your whole group by using the icebreaker question(s), or you can check in with one or two group members—your spiritual partner(s)—for a deeper connection and encouragement in your spiritual journey.

As your group begins, use the Small Group Agreement and Small Group Calendar to help your group see how everyone has a part in making a small group come to life. As the group develops intimacy, use the Spiritual Partner's Check-In Page and Prayer and Praise Report to keep the group connected.

Learning Together/DVD TEACHING SEGMENT.

Serving as a companion to *Your Extraordinary Life* small group discussion book is *Your Extraordinary Life* Video teaching. This DVD is designed to combine teaching segments from Pastor Allen Jackson along with leadership insights and personal stories of life change. Using the teaching video will add value to this 6-week commitment of doing life together and discovering how walking with Christ allows ordinary people to live extraordinary lives. (NOTE: Questions with a * indicate the crucial ones to use if time is short)

Growing Together.

In this section you will process as a group the teaching you heard and saw. The focus won't be on accumulating information but on how we should live in light of the Word of God. We want to help you apply the insights from Scripture practically, creatively, and from your heart as well as your head. At the end of the day, allowing the timeless truths from God's Word to transform our lives in Christ is our greatest aim.

Deeper Bible Study.

If you have time and want to dig deeper into more Bible passages about the topic at hand, we've provided additional passages and questions. Your group may choose to do study homework ahead of each meeting in order to cover more biblical material. If you prefer not to do study homework, the Deeper Bible Study section will provide you with plenty to discuss within the group. These options allow individuals or the whole group to expand their study, while still accommodating those who can't do homework or are new to your group.

Sharing Together.

We let the truth we are learning travel the 18 inches from our cranium (mind) to our cardium (heart, emotions, and will). This is where the Bible urges us to "be doers of the Word, not just hearers" (James 1:22) comes into play. Many people skip over this aspect of the Christian life because it's scary, relationally awkward, or simply too much work for their busy schedules. But Jesus wanted all of his disciples to help outsiders connect with him, to know him personally, and to carry out his commands. This doesn't necessarily mean preaching on street corners. It could mean welcoming a few newcomers into your group, hosting a short-term group in your home, or walking through this study with a friend. In this study, you'll have an opportunity to go beyond Bible study to biblical living.

Going Together.

We have Jesus' affirmation that every aspect of life can ultimately be measured as a way of fulfilling one or both of the "bottom line" commandment: *"The most important one," answered Jesus, "is this: 'Hear, O Israel, the Lord our God, the Lord is one. Love the Lord your God with all your heart and with all your soul and with all your mind and with all your strength.' The second is this: 'Love your neighbor as yourself.' There is no commandment greater than these"* (Mark 12:29–31 NIV). The group session will close with time for personal response to God and group prayer, seeking to keep this crucial commandment before us at all times.

This is a good place to have different group members close in prayer, even when the instructions don't specify. You can also provide some time if the schedule allows for people to reflect on their Prayer and Praise Report or take a little time to meet with a Spiritual Partner.

Daily Devotionals.

Each week on the Daily Devotionals pages we provide scriptures to read and reflect on between group meetings. We suggest you use this section to seek God on your own throughout the week. This time at home should begin and end with prayer. Don't get in a hurry; take enough time to hear God's direction.

Weekly Memory Verse.

For each session we have provided a Memory Verse that emphasizes an important truth from the session. This is an optional exercise, but we believe that memorizing Scripture can be a vital part of filling our minds with God's will for our lives. We encourage you to give this important habit a try.

SESSION 1
Life Ordinary or Extraordinary?

Welcome

to *Your Extraordinary Life*! Enjoy the company around you on this brief journey and remember that it's a small chapter in a larger story God is writing in your life. Let's discover together what it means to live such a remarkable life and what steps we can take to make sure that's the life we're living.

Charlie Daniels

"If you don't love it, you ain't gonna do it." That's how Charlie Daniels describes learning to play the guitar, but it says a lot about one of the keys to living *Your Extraordinary Life*. It's not really a question about hard or easy things…we will run into both. *Your Extraordinary Life* flows partly out of finding what you love to do and then doing it for as long as you can.

Charles Edward "Charlie" Daniels (born on October 28, 1936) is an American musician known for his contributions to country and southern rock music. Vocals, guitar, fiddle, bass are his primary vehicles, along with songwriting. He admits that the music part of his vocation doesn't come instinctively or naturally. He describes with amazement how some of his band companions seem to effortlessly play music that he really has to work at. Watch for his appreciation of the skills of those around him. And as we will see, Charlie does have a way with words.

He is perhaps best known for his number one country hit "The Devil Went Down to Georgia", and multiple other songs he has written and performed. Daniels has been active as a singer since the early 1950s. He was inducted into the Grand Ole Opry

on January 24, 2008. Even though, as he tells it, he had played the Grand Ole Opry countless times in his career, being recognized and invited to join was an amazing affirmation after fifty years pursuing his love for music.

In a way that fits someone who not long ago wrote a heartfelt cry called "Simple Man," a song about the conditions he sees in society around him, Charlie gives the credit to God for the good things in the life he has lived. He has sought to give attention to God in all his ways, and, as Charlie describes it, "God has given the desires of my heart in ways I could not have anticipated." He recognizes with gratitude that he is a blessed man. He also has some important things to say about moving from a casual, foggy faith to a vital relationship with God that understands what Christ has done for us.

Charlie knows that at the center of an authentic extraordinary life is always an extraordinary God.

COMING TOGETHER

During each session, we will begin with a question or brief activity designed to "put us on the same page" for the session. Since this is your first time together (at least for this new series), take a few minutes to make sure everyone knows names. You may want to review briefly the Small Group Agreement and Calendar from the Appendix.

1 As you begin, take time to pass around a copy of the Small Group Roster on page 113, a sheet of paper, or one of you pass your Study Guide, opened to the Small Group Roster. Have everyone write down their contact information. Ask someone to make copies or type up a list with everyone's information and email it to the group this week.

2 Pastor Allen likes to remind us he grew up in a barn. Let's take a few minutes and discover some of the common and perhaps unusual places the people in our small group grew up. What's the most unusual thing you can tell us about your early years?

3 Describe a choice that you made at least ten years ago that you believe has made a big difference in your life?

4 Can you remember the first time you heard the song "The Devil Went Down to Georgia"? Where were you?

Notes:

LEARNING TOGETHER

Throughout the sessions in *Your Extraordinary Life* we're hearing some pointed teaching from Pastor Allen Jackson as well as some personal stories from ordinary people who have lived extraordinary lives. Our lives may be significantly different in background and opportunity from others, but we can choose to live the extraordinary life God has designed for us. With that possibility in mind, let's begin our teaching for this session:

DVD SESSION 1

Use the space provided below for any notes, questions, or comments you want to bring up in the discussion later.

_____

_____

_____

_____

GROWING TOGETHER

In the questions that follow, you will review and expand on the teaching you just experienced.

5 What do you think would happen where you work if you went in tomorrow and said, "By the way, I was at a small group yesterday and Charlie Daniels and Allen Jackson showed up"?

6 Pastor Allen mentioned LeBron James, Bill Gates, Donald Trump...as people some might envy or compare themselves to as paragons of the extraordinary life. What are some other examples that come to mind? Do you think we're better off simply appreciating what these people have done or wishing we could take their place? Why?

7 *This session was about three ideas to believe in that will affect how you experience the rest of the study. The first concept was: God has put the power of choice in your hands. How would you explain that idea to someone who wasn't here?

8 *According to Galatians 5:1, *"It is for freedom that Christ has set us free. Stand firm, then, and do not let yourselves be burdened again by a yoke of slavery."* (NIV) When you hear a statement like, "Christianity is about freedom!" how do you respond?

9 *Concept two was about the significance of *preferences* and individuality in God's plan. What difference does it make to realize you can only live your life, not anyone else's?

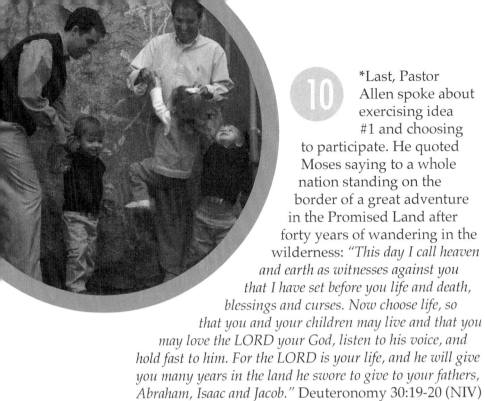

10 *Last, Pastor Allen spoke about exercising idea #1 and choosing to participate. He quoted Moses saying to a whole nation standing on the border of a great adventure in the Promised Land after forty years of wandering in the wilderness: *"This day I call heaven and earth as witnesses against you that I have set before you life and death, blessings and curses. Now choose life, so that you and your children may live and that you may love the LORD your God, listen to his voice, and hold fast to him. For the LORD is your life, and he will give you many years in the land he swore to give to your fathers, Abraham, Isaac and Jacob."* Deuteronomy 30:19-20 (NIV) List two or three of the best choices you've made in your life.

11 If *Your Extraordinary Life* is ultimately a life that displays the uniqueness God designed in each of us, what does it take to participate in an extraordinary life? Is it more about finding/getting something new and "superhuman" or is it about realizing how God made you from the start? Why?

GOING DEEPER

You can explore the following Bible passages behind the teaching for this session as a group (if there is time) or on your own between sessions.

Read Psalm 139:13-18.

In this entire Psalm, David examines both his relationship with God and the amazing evidence of God's care for him.

What does it mean to admit to God that He has "fearfully and wonderfully made" us?

How does it affect a person's relationship with God to realize, as Pastor Allen put it, "God doesn't make any junk!"?

So if God made us fearfully and wonderfully, how do you think He wants to be involved in our participation in an extraordinary life?

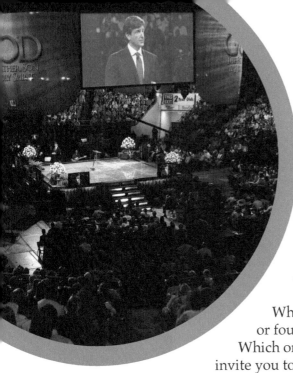

Read Deuteronomy 30:11-20.

Moses is wrapping up a long sermon (the whole book of Deuteronomy), reminding the people of everything they have seen God do for them. Now he wants them to make the choice and participate!

What would you say are the three or four key words in this passage? Which ones keep your attention and invite you to engage?

Summarize the main point of each section of these passages: Deuteronomy 11-14; 15-16; 17-18; 19-20. How do these main points highlight Moses' challenge?

How would you explain the common thread between the phrase "choose life" in verse 19 and the phrase "For the LORD is your life" in verse 20? What does this tell us about the authentic extraordinary life?

SHARING TOGETHER

Now it's time to make some personal applications to all we've been thinking about in the last few minutes.

*When you think about Pastor Allen's three main points, (1-God gives us power to choose; 2-God creates us individually, and 3-God invites us to participate with Him), which one of these do you find hardest to accept or to put into practice? Why?

If you could put into words one new personal idea or challenge you are taking from this session, what would it be? How did the interview with Charlie Daniels impact your understanding of an extraordinary life?

GOING TOGETHER

During these sessions we are doing things "together:" learning, thinking, growing, praying, choosing, etc. Part of together is how we live when we aren't together. Here are some questions to clarify our shared purposes until we meet again.

14 Pastor Allen ended his teaching with the challenge to think of others we might invite to join us for these sessions. If someone came to mind, write their name(s) here:

15 *What's one choice you can make this week (and share with the group) that you believe would move you toward a more authentic and extraordinary life?

16 *Allow everyone to answer this question: "How can we pray for you this week?" Be sure to write prayer requests on your Prayer and Praise Report on page 112.

DAILY REFLECTIONS

Day 1

Galatians 5:1 | Real Freedom

It is for freedom that Christ has set us free. Stand firm, then, and do not let yourselves be burdened again by a yoke of slavery. (NIV)

<u>**Reflection Question:**</u> What's the difference in your life between Christ setting you free and the way you live freely? Where does "slavery" still try to yoke you?

Day 2

John 10:10 | An Extraordinary Life

The thief comes only to steal and kill and destroy; I have come that they may have life, and have it to the full. (NIV)

<u>**Reflection Question:**</u> In what sense do you consider your life "full" as Jesus called it? What "thieves" have you experienced in life?

Day 3

Genesis 1:31 | Made Good

God saw all that he had made, and it was very good. And there was eve-ning, and there was morning—the sixth day. (NIV)

Reflection Question: Even before you met Christ, what clues did you have that God had given you a life that was good?

Day 4

John 14:6 | Real Life

Jesus answered, "I am the way and the truth and the life. No one comes to the Father except through me." (NIV)

Reflection Question: If life in Jesus is the extraordinary life, then what part does Jesus as the way and Jesus as the truth affect your daily choices?

Matthew 16:25 | Finding an Extraordinary Life

For whoever wants to save his life will lose it, but whoever loses his life for me will find it. What good will it be for a man if he gains the whole world, yet forfeits his soul? Or what can a man give in exchange for his soul? (NIV)

<u>Reflection Question:</u> How ready would you say you are to choose God's way of living an extraordinary life in place of living by the standards set by anyone else (including yourself)?

Weekly Memory Verse

God saw all that he had made, and it was very good. And there was evening, and there was morning—the sixth day. (Genesis 1:31 NIV)

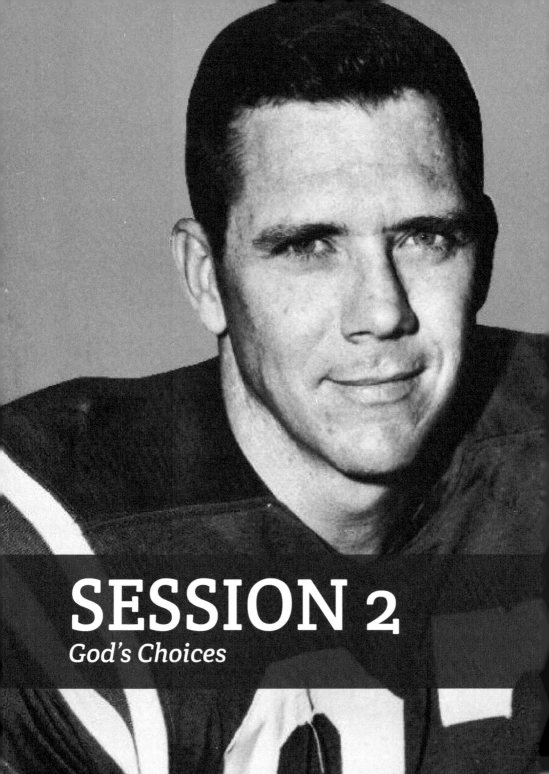

SESSION 2

God's Choices

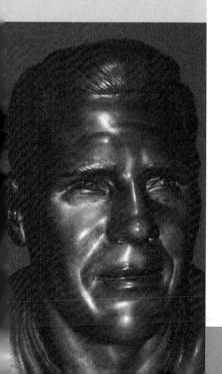

Raymond Emmett Berry

(born February 27, 1933) is a former football wide receiver. He played for the Baltimore Colts during their two NFL championship wins. He later had a career in coaching, highlighted by his trip to Super Bowl XX as head coach of the New England Patriots. He is a member of the Pro Football Hall of Fame.

During his career, Berry led the NFL in receptions three times. He was selected to the Pro Bowl six times, from 1957–61 and in 1965. He also made the all-NFL team from 1958-1960. He was famous for his attention to detail and preparation. He and Baltimore Colts quarterback John Unitas regularly worked after practice and developed the timing and knowledge of each other's abilities that made each more effective. In addition to his great record as a pass receiver, Berry's dedication to his craft is demonstrated by, in a 13-year career, his fumbling the football only once — though some would say this was really an incomplete pass.

Raymond Berry ended his NFL career in 1967 with an NFL record 631 receptions for 9,275 yards and 68 touchdowns (14.7 yards per catch). In 1973, Berry was voted into the Pro

Football Hall of Fame in Canton, Ohio. In 1999, he was ranked No. 40 on The Sporting News' list of the 100 Greatest Football Players.

On February 5, 2012, Berry (with his strong ties to both teams playing in Super Bowl XLVI, the Giants and the Patriots) presented the Vince Lombardi Trophy to NFL commissioner Roger Goodell, who awarded it to Super Bowl MVP Eli Manning.

COMING TOGETHER

During each session, we will begin with a question or brief activity designed to "put us on the same page" for the session. Continue to make sure everyone knows names.

1 Somewhere in your life is an ice cream store with a mind-boggling, sweet-tooth challenging, taste tempting variety of flavors to choose from. Given that smorgasbord of frozen delights, what do you choose for your treat?

2 On behalf of those who might be joining us for the first time this session, what lasting idea from the last session has been on your mind this past week that would you be willing to mention to the rest of the group?

LEARNING TOGETHER

Throughout the sessions in *Your Extraordinary Life* we're hearing some pointed teaching from Pastor Allen Jackson as well as some personal stories from ordinary people who have lived extraordinary lives. Our lives may be significantly different in background and opportunity from others, but we can choose to live the extraordinary life God has designed for us. With that possibility in mind, let's begin our teaching for this session:

DVD SESSION 2

Use the space provided below for any notes, questions, or comments you want to bring up in the discussion later.

GROWING TOGETHER

In the questions that follow, you will review and expand on the teaching you just experienced.

3 In what ways do you think Raymond Berry is a great example of what it means to live an extraordinary life?

4 How did you respond to and how would you explain Pastor Allen's statement early in the teaching that his desire is "not to be more churched or more religious, but to be more and more about living an extraordinary life"?

5 *Let's look again at the verses from the New Testament that Pastor Allen read:

The God who made the world and everything in it is the Lord of heaven and earth and does not live in temples built by hands. And he is not served by human hands, as if he needed anything, because <u>he himself gives all men life and breath and everything else</u>. From one man he made every nation of men, that they should inhabit the whole earth; and <u>he determined the times</u> set for them and <u>the exact places</u>

where they should live. God did this so that men would seek him and perhaps reach out for him and find him, though he is not far from each one of us. 'For in him we live and move and have our being.' As some of your own poets have said, 'We are his offspring.' Acts 17:24-28 (NIV - underline added)

6 *The first underlined phrase in the verse is that God gives life, breath, and everything else. Did God withhold anything you need to be extraordinary? Do we have faith to agree with God?

7 *Pastor Allen noted the use of the word *times* in the second underlined phrase in the verse above has to do with seasons or periods—not just the clock. What comforts or challenges do you think we can draw from being alive at a season like today, especially if God arranged it?

8 If God chose the places for you to live, how would that impact your responses?

9 Think for a moment about Allen's definition of disappointments: "An appointment you didn't make or wouldn't have made!" How do you find this helpful?

GOING DEEPER

You can explore the following Bible passages behind the teaching for this session as a group (if there is time) or on your own between sessions.

Read Ecclesiastes 3:1-14.

Solomon doesn't just talk about times; he says there's "a time" for many of the significant parts of life. There's a certain order, pattern, and sequence to living.

How many times is God mentioned in this passage, and what does it tell us about Him?

What are some of the things (like raising kids) that must be done in a certain time rather than when we get around to them? Why is it important to remember this?

In what ways does it make sense to you that "God does it [all of the above] so that men will revere him" (v.14)? How would you describe "revering" God?

Read Acts 17:16-33.

Paul has been wandering around Athens and eventually begins to preach on a corner and gets invited to the main stage. He's speaking to the top intellectuals in Greek society of his time.

Where in these verses do we find Paul describing part of God's purpose in the way He created human beings?

Athens in Paul's day was the ultimate pluralistic society, with gods everywhere. Why do you think he approached them with something he noticed in their own approach to religion? Do you see anything similar in our society where religion is everywhere but rarely makes a significant difference in our lives?

Paul's sermon ended with a "split decision" by his audience. What does this tell us about the kinds of responses we make to the offer of an extraordinary life?

SHARING TOGETHER

Now it's time to make some personal applications to all we've been thinking about in the last few minutes.

10 *What did you find personally challenging or motivating about the interview with Raymond Berry that began this session?

11 How would you describe the one thing that you find most exciting or encouraging about pursuing an extraordinary life?

12 *If disappointments (by definition) aren't predictable and in many ways unavoidable, what would be one thing you've seen in those who live extraordinary lives that carries them through disappointments and setbacks?

GOING TOGETHER

During these sessions we are doing things "together:" learning, thinking, growing, praying, choosing, etc. Part of "together" is how we live when we aren't together. Here are some questions to clarify our shared purposes until we meet again.

What's one idea from this session you plan to talk about with someone beyond this group this week? Why?

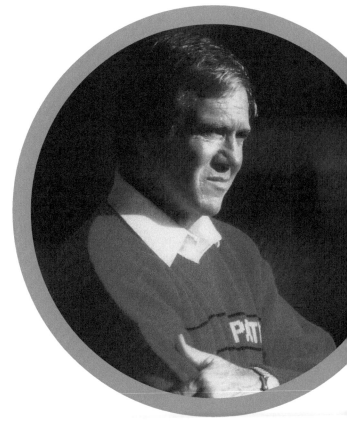

14 *Pair up with someone in your group. (We suggest that men partner with men and women with women.) This person will be your spiritual partner for the rest of this study. He or she doesn't have to be your best friend, but will simply encourage you to complete the goals you set for yourself during this study. Following through on a resolution is tough when you're on your own, but we've found it makes all the difference to have a partner cheering us on.

15 *As he closed his teaching, Pastor Allen invited us to pray with him a prayer of yielding to God's purposes in our lives. Let's pray the following prayer together as a way to prepare ourselves for the days to come:

Father, thank You for the choices You've made in my life, regarding who I am, what I'm going through, and where I'm going through it! Thank You that You never leave me or forsake me. Thank You that I don't have to understand all the hows and whys but that You can create an extraordinary life in me. That's exactly what I want to go for with everything I've got…in Jesus' name, Amen!

DAILY REFLECTIONS

Day 1

Ecclesiastes 3:1 | Keeping with the Times
There is a time for everything, and a season for every activity under heaven. (NIV)

Reflection Question: How would describe the main activities, responsibilities, and opportunities God has built into this time for you?

Day 2

Acts 17:27 | Sought Seekers
God did this so that men would seek him and perhaps reach out for him and find him, though he is not far from each one of us. (NIV)

Reflection Question: What is your earliest memory of sensing God was seeking you? How did He finally get your attention?

Day 3

Ecclesiastes 3:11 | Listening to Eternity

He has made everything beautiful in its time. He has also set eternity in the hearts of men; yet they cannot fathom what God has done from beginning to end. (NIV)

Reflection Question: In what sense do you identify with that phrase "eternity in the heart" in your life?

_____

_____

_____

_____

Day 4

Galatians 4:4 | Timing

But when the time had fully come, God sent his Son, born of a woman, born under law. (NIV)

Reflection Question: Pastor Allen talked about timing and placing in Jesus' life. Why might God have you where you are, doing what you do at this point in your life?

_____

_____

_____

_____

Day 5

Philippians 4:12-13 | Yielding to God's Purposes

*I know what it is to be in need, and I know what it is to have plenty.
I have learned the secret of being content in any and every situation,
whether well fed or hungry, whether living in plenty or in want. I can do
everything through him who gives me strength.* (NIV)

<u>Reflection Question:</u> In what areas of your life do you still need to
"learn the secret of being content" with God's choices?

_____

_____

_____

_____

Weekly Memory Verse

*God did this so that men
would seek him and perhaps
reach out for him and find
him, though he is not far
from each one of us.*
Acts 17:27 (NIV)

SESSION 3
Our Choices

It's hard not to chuckle when we realize that even the decision to think of life as something completely out of our control is itself an example of a choice we make. Choice is unavoidable. Yes, God has a lot to do with many things, but one of the things He does is give us choices. What we do with them makes all the difference between an ordinary, wasted, or extraordinary life.

George and Betty Jackson

have been actively involved in ministry for more than thirty years. They've known each other for more than sixty years, first as high school sweethearts and then as a young married couple. They are quick to dismiss ideas that their lasting marriage was due to their perfect match. Both of them admit to being determined, strong-willed people, willing to fight the good fight for what's important. And they used their determination to build a strong marriage and to serve the Lord Jesus Christ.

During her third pregnancy, Betty was diagnosed with cancer. That very difficult time was used by God to move the Jackson's from a casual awareness of God to a living trust in Him. Faced with the real possibility of life-ending sickness, the Jacksons had to apply an awakening need for God to their hope for the future. They now see how God used even the hard parts of these experiences to bring them to Himself.

George Jackson was trained in veterinary medicine and earned his doctorate from the University of Missouri School of Veterinary Medicine. His practice allowed the Jacksons an effective platform for practicing faith among the business community.

Their global efforts have included church planting, writing, and international outreach, with a special interest in the Middle East. The central theme in all their pursuits has been to help people find freedom through the power of Jesus Christ. But as is the case of many extraordinary lives, the early years are not necessarily an obvious foundation for the way God eventually uses those people. Just think about Moses leading sheep around the wilderness for forty years before he did another 40-year tour with people who were a lot harder to manage than sheep!

God's faithfulness in expanding their vision and ministry has been a consistent aspect of their faith journey. In the 70's they initiated a home Bible study in Murfreesboro which eventually led to the birth of World Outreach Church in 1980. As directors of Derek Prince Israel, George and Betty reside in Jerusalem half of each year and spend the other half teaching and giving pastoral care at World Outreach Church.

Today, the Jackson's eldest son, Allen, is senior pastor of the World Outreach Church in Murfreesboro, Tennessee, with their son Phillip as associate pastor. The couple's youngest son, Doyle, is pastor of The Church Next Door in Columbus, Ohio

COMING TOGETHER

During each session, we begin with a question or brief activity designed to "put us on the same page" for the session.

1 As we will see in the story of George and Betty Jackson, a marriage can be a great setting for an extraordinary life. As we begin this session, what married couple has had a significant influence on your life? How?

2 On behalf of those who might be joining us for the first time this session, who would like to describe one significant discovery you've made in the last two sessions of *Your Extraordinary Life*?

3 We also suggest you rotate providing refreshments to support the host home. The Small Group Calendar on page 109 is a tool for planning who will host and lead each meeting.

LEARNING TOGETHER

Throughout the sessions in *Your Extraordinary Life* we're hearing some pointed teaching from Pastor Allen Jackson as well as some personal stories from ordinary people who have lived extraordinary lives. Our lives may be significantly different in background and opportunity from others, but we can choose to live the extraordinary life God has designed for us. With that possibility in mind, let's begin our teaching for this session:

DVD SESSION 3

Use the space provided below for any notes, questions, or comments you want to bring up in the discussion later.

GROWING TOGETHER

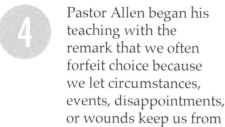

In the questions that follow, you will review and expand on the teaching you just experienced.

4 Pastor Allen began his teaching with the remark that we often forfeit choice because we let circumstances, events, disappointments, or wounds keep us from making decisions that could lead to extraordinary living. How have you observed this kind of self-limitation in your life?

5 *Do you agree or disagree with this statement: God has already given you everything you need to live your extraordinary life? Why or why not?

6 *You can choose to participate in the Kingdom of God. How do we enter God's Kingdom?

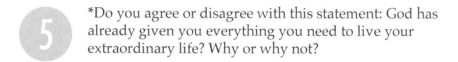

7 *Romans 10:9 is the basis for a prayer that brings about the birth God longs to do in and for us? Let's pray this prayer aloud together. If you've prayed this prayer before, use this as a tool to help someone else be birthed into the Kingdom.

God I am a sinner and I need a Savior. I believe Jesus is your Son, that He died on a Cross for me and that you raised Him to life again that I might be justified. Jesus I ask you to be Lord of my life. I want to live for Your glory. I want to live for Your honor. I want to serve you. Amen.

8 *What are the components of spiritual health that Pastor Allen mentioned in his second suggestion?

9 *Deciding to get married happens in a moment; deciding to be married is a daily commitment. How does this work out in following Jesus and the principle of spiritual maturity that was Pastor Allen's third suggestion in this session?

GOING DEEPER

You can explore the following Bible passages behind the teaching for this session as a group (if there is time) or on your own between sessions.

Read Ephesians 4:1-16.

Paul has shifted his focus from the crucial subject of all that we have in Christ (Chapters 1-3) to his urging the Ephesians and us to *"in all things grow up into him who is the Head, that is, Christ"* (v.15).

Verses 2-3 mention five basic character traits of a Christ-follower's worthy life. How many of them require the involvement of others in some way in order for us to grow? How many can we develop on our own?

What do verses 11-13 describe the role of leaders in the church in relation to spiritual development of believers?

Particularly in verses 14-16 but throughout this passage, how many examples can you find of Paul's emphasis on growing to spiritual maturity?

Read Jeremiah 9:23-24.

We all understand that there's knowing and there's *knowing*. Knowing a subject matter or a skill is something quite different than knowing a person. When it comes to God, acquiring factual knowledge (knowing about Him), is going to create different results in our lives compared to knowing Him intimately and personally.

What three personal achievements do these verses list that tend to be the subject of our conversation and quest for meaning?

Can you think of any other boast-prone areas that we sometimes use to try to make our lives significant?

How does this passage describe what it means to know God in such a way that we're willing to talk about that relationship even when it might seem like boasting to others? What experiences in knowing God this way have already been part of your life?

SHARING TOGETHER

Now it's time to make some personal applications to all we've been thinking about in the last few minutes.

 As Pastor Allen made clear in talking about his first suggestion, every long term commitment starts with a decision. A relationship with God starts with a kingdom decision, God welcome us to the Kingdom of His Son. How has the decision to be a Christ-follower changed your life?

11 Of the three stages Pastor Allen covered in his teaching (The Kingdom Decision, the Spiritual Health Decisions, and the Spiritual Maturity Decisions), which one most closely relates to your own spiritual situation right now?

GOING TOGETHER

During these sessions we are doing things "together:" learning, thinking, growing, praying, choosing, etc. Part of together is how we live when we aren't together. Here are some questions to clarify our shared purposes until we meet again.

12 When you think of your present relationship with Christ, how can the rest of the group be praying for you this week as you seek to give yourself more fully to God's plan for your extraordinary life?

13 What experiences have you had in talking with others outside the group about what we are studying together during these sessions?

Close the session in prayer. Encourage each other to pray for others in the group.

Notes:

DAILY REFLECTIONS

Day 1

John 3:3 | The Birth Decision

In reply Jesus declared, "I tell you the truth, no one can see the kingdom of God unless he is born again." (NIV)

Reflection Question: "Born again" has become a cliché in our culture, but what reality was Jesus really talking about and how have your experienced it?

_____

_____

_____

_____

Day 2

Ephesians 4:15-16 | Body Life

Instead, speaking the truth in love, we will in all things grow up into him who is the Head, that is, Christ. From him the whole body, joined and held together by every supporting ligament, grows and builds itself up in love, as each part does its work. (NIV)

Reflection Question: What was the last evidence of specific spiritual growth in your life within the body of Christ?

_____

_____

_____

Day 3

Mark 2:17 | Spiritual Check-up

On hearing this, Jesus said to them, "It is not the healthy who need a doctor, but the sick. I have not come to call the righteous, but sinners." (NIV)

Reflection Question: When was the last time you had a spiritual health check-up with Jesus? What was His diagnosis and treatment plan for you?

_____

_____

_____

_____

Day 4

Psalm 19:12-14 | Examination

Who can discern his errors? Forgive my hidden faults. Keep your servant also from willful sins; may they not rule over me. Then will I be blameless, innocent of great transgression. May the words of my mouth and the meditation of my heart be pleasing in your sight, O LORD, my Rock and my Redeemer. (NIV)

Reflection Question: Use this passage as a prayer, asking God to reveal to you areas that He wants to work on in your life. What is He telling you?

_____

_____

_____

_____

Day 5

John 16:1, 33 | Lovingly Warned

All this I have told you so that you will not go astray….
I have told you these things, so that in me you may have peace. In this world
you will have trouble. But take heart! I have overcome the world. (NIV)

<u>**Reflection Question:**</u> In what ways do these verses help you
deepen your understanding that following Jesus
is for a lifetime and beyond?

Instead, speaking the truth in love, we will in all things grow up into him who is the Head, that is, Christ. From him the whole body, joined and held together by every supporting ligament, grows and builds itself up in love, as each part does its work.
Ephesians 4:15-16 (NIV)

SESSION 4
Overcoming Disappointment

session we should
be settling into a
level of comfort
with the group,
continuing to
welcome any
newcomers. In
this session we'll
be taking a look
at bumps in the
road—sometimes
big potholes—that
set us back, knock
us down, or slow us
up, but don't have to
stop us in our tracks.

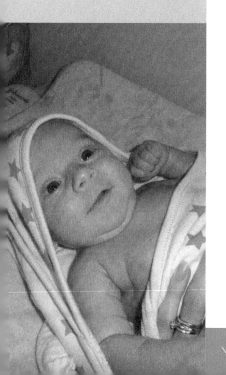

Krystn Drummond

Krystn as well as her husband Ryan are California natives. They ended up in the Nashville area as a result of Krystn's developing musical career. They have been an active part of World Outreach Church for a number of years. They are a perfect example of how life can seem to the observer to be ideal in many ways when from the inside it looks like one daunting challenge after another.

It's almost impossible to imagine the struggle facing a parent whose child is suffering from a sickness or disability. The helplessness is overwhelming. Disappointments stack up like cordwood, and it often appears there is no end in sight. But Krystn Drummond reminds us that we can trust a God who works miracles and one of the first ones He often does is give us the strength to keep going one more step, one more day.

In Krystn and in particular her daughter Natalie's case, a miracle came in the form of an unexplainable (except by the power of God) healing from debilitating seizures from birth. Not only was Natalie healed, but Krystn and her husband were given a little brother for Natalie who is whole against the odds.

Krystn's story is the account of a woman facing more than she could handle and discovering that God was with her every step of the way. It's not that some days were hard and many were impossible; it's that God makes things possible that can't be done or explained any other way.

She reminds us that disappointments and setbacks really are a part of living in a challenging world, and overcoming them requires us to learn to trust and depend on God in ever-increasing ways. And watch for miracles along the way, too.

COMING TOGETHER

During each session, we will begin with a question or brief activity designed to "put us on the same page" for the session. Continue to make sure everyone knows names.

1. Think for a moment about all the delayed gratification that we experience in cooking and eating—waiting for the catsup to pour, the pot to boil, the dough to rise, and the toast to jump. Which of these (or another that comes to mind) is hardest for you to wait for? Why?

2. If you've been with us in previous sessions, Pastor Allen has already mentioned the fact that disappointments play into extraordinary lives just like they play into all lives. Obstacles and disappointments are part of our journey. Briefly explain a personal experience of perseverance.

LEARNING TOGETHER

Throughout the sessions in *Your Extraordinary Life* we're hearing some pointed teaching from Pastor Allen Jackson as well as some personal stories from ordinary people who have lived extraordinary lives. Our lives may be significantly different in background and opportunity from others, but we can choose to live the extraordinary life God has designed for us. With that possibility in mind, let's begin our teaching for this session:

DVD SESSION 4

Use the space provided below for any notes, questions, or comments you want to bring up in the discussion later.

_____

_____

_____

_____

GROWING TOGETHER

In the questions that follow, you will review and expand on the teaching you just experienced.

3 Nothing like listening to an experience like Krystn's to put our own trials into different light! What do you take away from her story?

4 For some of us Daniel may be a stranger or vague ancient figure. Pooling our group knowledge, what do we know about Daniel, whose story is told in the Old Testament in the book by the same name?

5 *Pastor Allen reminds us that when we meet Daniel, the circumstances in his life were "less than ideal—hideous in fact." Why do you think that almost every heroic person we meet in the Bible has at least one significant disappointment or setback to negotiate on the way to an extraordinary life?

6 *The teaching included a working definition of an extraordinary life: *An ordinary person (in the middle of the mundane, ups and downs of daily experience) who cooperates with God and lets something extraordinary emerge from their life.* Identify circumstances where you have included God. What has been the impact? Reflect upon times you were reluctant to include God's perspective. What has been the impact?

7 *Two summary statements are made about Daniel when he had already lived a lengthy life, the first by the queen of Babylon, the second by a messenger of God:

1. *There is a man in your kingdom in whom is a spirit of the holy gods; and in the days of your father, illumination, insight and wisdom like the wisdom of the gods were found in him. And King Nebuchadnezzar, your father, your father the king, appointed him chief of the magicians, conjurers, Chaldeans and diviners. This was because an extraordinary spirit, knowledge and insight, interpretation of dreams, explanation of enigmas and solving of difficult problems were found in this Daniel, whom the king named Belteshazzar. Let Daniel now be summoned and he will declare the interpretation.*" (Daniel 5:11-12, NASB)

2. He said, *"Daniel, you who are highly esteemed, consider carefully the words I am about to speak to you, and stand up, for I have now been sent to you." And when he said this to me, I stood up trembling.*

Then he continued, *"Do not be afraid, Daniel. Since the first day that you set your mind to gain understanding and to humble yourself before your God, your words were heard, and I have come in response to them."* (Daniel 10:11-12 NIV)

What do these two statements tell you about the effects of Daniel's choices?

8 Using Daniel, we are reminded that life brings great difficulties and disappointments along with the joys and triumphs. Cultivating God's character within us through repentance, humility and the fear of the Lord we are able to thrive in all seasons. What have you learned about yourself and God in difficult seasons?

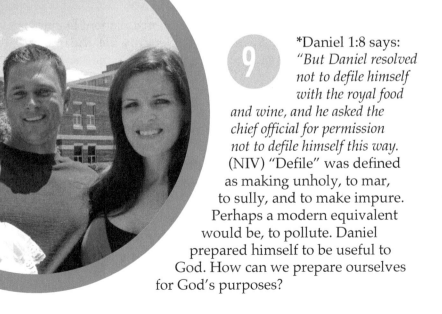

9 *Daniel 1:8 says: "But Daniel resolved not to defile himself with the royal food and wine, and he asked the chief official for permission not to defile himself this way.* (NIV) "Defile" was defined as making unholy, to mar, to sully, and to make impure. Perhaps a modern equivalent would be, to pollute. Daniel prepared himself to be useful to God. How can we prepare ourselves for God's purposes?

GOING DEEPER

You can explore the following Bible passages behind the teaching for this session as a group (if there is time) or on your own between sessions.

Read Daniel 3:1-30.

Daniel's friends had their own episode with the temptation to defile themselves through compromise and failure to trust God. It was a life or death test of faith.

Why did it matter to these three men that they not bow down and worship Nebuchadnezzar's statue?

How does their faith demonstrate extraordinary realism in the face of a death threat in verses 16-18?

What kinds of challenges might we face today in which we would be called to demonstrate a similar stand for God in the face of pressure to conform or compromise?

Read Mark 7:1-23.

The religious people of Jesus' time had a twisted view of defilement. They micromanaged the obvious and ignored the blatant. Then they made the mistake of confronting and accusing Jesus and His disciples of defiling themselves.

How would you describe the details of this confrontation? What were the charges against the disciples?

What was Jesus' main response and what examples did He use to make His case?

When He was alone with the disciples, how did Jesus expand on the teaching about clean and unclean?

In what ways is Jesus' description of our lives a profound statement of timeless truth?

SHARING TOGETHER

Now it's time to make some personal applications to all we've been thinking about in the last few minutes.

10 Why is it so difficult for many of us to make, what Pastor Allen calls, "The decision to honor God to the best of our knowledge?" And when we make that decision, what makes it survive more than a day or two?

11 *In whatever season of life we find ourselves, if we decide to make godliness our best path forward, God Himself will respond. Is there a specific decision you are prepared to yield to God's way? Explain.

12 What current or possible disappointment/setback/challenge are you facing that may give you a chance to practice honoring God this week? How can the rest of us pray for you?

13 Who in your life right now might you encourage with the hopeful message you're taking away from this session? If God gives you an opportunity, what do you want to tell them?

GOING TOGETHER

During these sessions we are doing things "together:" learning, thinking, growing, praying, choosing, etc. Part of together is how we live when we aren't together. Here are some questions to clarify our shared purposes until we meet again.

14 Each of you share how you have done with inviting people church or your small group.

15 Check in with your spiritual partner(s), or with another partner if yours is absent. Share something God taught you during your time in His Word this week, or read a brief section from your journal. Be sure to write down your partner's progress on page 110.

Close the session in prayer. Encourage each other to pray for others in the group.

DAILY REFLECTIONS

Day 1

1 Timothy 4:8 | The Pursuit of Godliness

For physical training is of some value, but godliness has value for all things, holding promise for both the present life and the life to come. (NIV)

Reflection Question: What is your current understanding of godliness and how is it challenged or confirmed by these sessions?

_____

_____

_____

_____

Day 2

Daniel 1:8 | Resolved

But Daniel resolved not to defile himself with the royal food and wine, and he asked the chief official for permission not to defile himself this way. (NIV)

Reflection Question: What's the difference between Daniel's resolution and what we usually call resolutions?

_____

_____

_____

Day 3

Matthew 25:21 | Well Done

His master replied, "Well done, good and faithful servant! You have been faithful with a few things; I will put you in charge of many things. Come and share your master's happiness!" (NIV)

Reflection Question: What affect are these sessions having on you in awakening the possibility of hearing God say this to you at the end of your life?

Day 4

Daniel 1:17 | The Blessing of Godliness

To these four young men God gave knowledge and understanding of all kinds of literature and learning. And Daniel could understand visions and dreams of all kinds. (NIV)

Reflection Question: What blessings in your own life can be traced back to decisions about godliness?

Day 5

2 Corinthians 4:7-9 | Clay Jars

But we have this treasure in jars of clay to show that this all-surpassing power is from God and not from us. We are hard pressed on every side, but not crushed; perplexed, but not in despair; persecuted, but not abandoned; struck down, but not destroyed. (NIV)

<u>Reflection Question:</u> How does Paul help us recognize that faithfulness isn't measured by the setbacks and difficulties in our lives?

_____

_____

_____

_____

Weekly Memory Verse

But Daniel resolved not to defile himself with the royal food and wine, and he asked the chief official for permission not to defile himself this way. Daniel 1:8 (NIV)

SESSION 5

Thriving in Crisis

Whether we are looking at a life three thousand years ago like Daniel's or a life sixty years ago like Johanna Hedges', crises are a reality at some point in everyone's life. For most of us the crucial question becomes, if the crisis hasn't happened yet, are we prepared?

Johanna Hedges

was a Jewish child born out of wedlock and adopted by Danish missionary Lydia Christensen. Lydia later married Derek Prince. Johanna lived her early life in the tumultuous days before the birth of the State of Israel, when Britain controlled much of the Middle East. The flow of Jewish refugees from the developing tensions in Europe before World War II and from Russia even before that had created quite a mixed society in Palestine. Lydia was living in Palestine at the time, called by God to care for abandoned children.

The Ramallah that Johanna remembers as a child was idyllic setting, where Arab, Jewish, and British children played together largely unaware of the crisis unfolding around the globe and the way it would greatly affect their lives. Johanna shared a family with girls from Jewish and Arab families gathered from many cities and social settings, more than 70 girls would be a part of their home. Later, Derek Prince joined the family as a father the girls needed.

Yet in all of the tumult that affected Johanna's life and could have left her traumatized, the strong sense of her connection with a family and the place God held in her life and the lives of those around her carried her through

difficult times. She became a woman of faith as God worked through the example of an adopted mother and father who practiced faith in a public as well as private way. She has lived an extraordinary life as the daughter of extraordinary lives!

Lydia Prince

COMING TOGETHER

During each session, we will begin with a question or brief activity designed to "put us on the same page" for the session. Continue to make sure everyone knows names.

1 Describe one skill or approach to life that you regularly use today that you know was shaped and developed when you were young.

2 What global level crisis would you say has most affected your life? Why?

George, Johanna and Stephen

LEARNING TOGETHER

Throughout the sessions in *Your Extraordinary Life* we're going to be hearing some pointed teaching from Pastor Allen Jackson as well as some personal stories from people who have lived extraordinary lives. We may not have the global range of personal and international crises that Johanna Hedges has experienced, but we can choose to live the extraordinary life God has designed for us. With that possibility in mind, let's begin our teaching for this session.

DVD SESSION 5

Use the space provided below for any notes, questions, or comments you want to bring up in the discussion later.

Lydia and her girls

GROWING TOGETHER

In the questions that follow, you will review and expand on the teaching you just experienced.

3 How would you describe a point in common that you have noticed about the life stories we've heard at the beginning of each teaching session in this series?

4 *Pastor Allen took us back to Daniel's story and in particular the statement in Daniel 5:11; *"There is a man in your kingdom who has the spirit of the holy gods in him. In the time of your father he was found to have insight and intelligence and wisdom like that of the gods."* (NIV) What point was Pastor Allen making when he said, "You can be that person to your friends, co-workers, and neighborhood"?

5 *In Daniel 5:17 we have his response to the offer of fabulous rewards and influence from the king in exchange for explaining the God writing on the wall: Then Daniel answered the king, *"You may keep your gifts for yourself and give your rewards to someone else. Nevertheless, I will read the writing for the king and tell him what it means."* (NIV) What core value was Daniel demonstrating?

6 *Pursuing God's best sometimes means saying no to personal ambition. Have you ever experienced this tension? Please describe this to the group.

7 *Pastor Allen pointed out that Daniel had a profound understanding of a covenant relationship with God that provides us with three significant crisis-management principles:

   a. Evil causes crises, and even the godly share the suffering.

   b. There's great value in regular 'time and place' aspects to our relationship with God.

   c. Preparation is never a waste of time and the arrival of a crisis is too late to prepare.

   Which of these principles do you find most helpful in understanding the way life unfolds? Why?

8 David prepared for Goliath, not because he knew he would go up against a giant sometime, but because he took seriously his responsibility to protect his flock from a lion or bear. Learning in one setting prepared him for another. How would you illustrate this truth from your own life?

GOING DEEPER

You can explore the following Bible passages behind the teaching for this session as a group (if there is time) or on your own between sessions.

Read Daniel 6:1-28.

Daniel was serving his third king when he faced a crisis created by others who were jealous of his role and determined to get rid of him. Daniel faced the lions unafraid.

What was the "Daniel problem" the other people in leadership had with Daniel that was on the agenda for their "get rid of Daniel" summit?

How did the administrators and satraps leverage Daniel's commitment to daily prayer and the king's commitment to his own integrity in order to succeed in their plan to eliminate Daniel?

How do Daniel 6:16 and 6:25-27 vindicate Daniel's approach to the plans of his enemies? How would even his death in the lion's den been an exclamation point on an extraordinary life?

Part of Daniels' covenant of time and place involved setting aside several times a day for prayer. What examples of time/place covenant are you pursuing in your relationship with God?

Read 1 Samuel 17:1-54.

Most of us know that David defeated Goliath. Where everyone else saw an enemy too big to challenge, David saw a target too big to miss! But the details of the story give us insights into the character of David that are worth knowing.

What was ultimately at stake in the conflict between Israel and the Philistines?

What fueled David's attitude toward Goliath and how was he misunderstood?

By leaving Saul's armor behind and taking only his sling to face the giant, what was David saying about his relationship to God?

SHARING TOGETHER

Now it's time to make some personal applications to all we've been thinking about in the last few minutes.

9   What examples can you think of from Johanna's story where earlier preparation allowed her to overcome later difficulties?

10   *What routines could you develop which would strengthen your spiritual life?

11   *As you make progress in honoring God with your life, what have been some the most visible impacts? What have you observed in others that you would like to cultivate?

GOING TOGETHER

During these sessions we are doing things "together:" learning, thinking, growing, praying, choosing, etc. Part of together is how we live when we aren't together. Here are some questions to clarify our shared purposes until we meet again.

 Since this is our next-to-last session in this series, what have we decided about next steps?

 In what ways would you say this experience has been helpful in preparing you to lead/host your own small group in the next series?

14 *Take a few minutes to discuss the future of your group. How many of you are willing to stay together as a group and work through another study together? If you have time, turn to the Small Group Agreement on page 108 and talk about any changes you would like to make as you move forward as a group.

Close the session in prayer. Encourage each other to pray for others in the group.

DAILY REFLECTIONS

Day 1

Daniel 5:11 | We're Watching You
There is a man in your kingdom who has the spirit of the holy gods in him. (NIV)

Reflection Question: Who's watching your life and how do you know it?

Day 2

Daniel 6:23 | God Glorified
The king was overjoyed and gave orders to lift Daniel out of the den. And when Daniel was lifted from the den, no wound was found on him, because he had trusted in his God. (NIV)

Reflection Question: On a scale of 1 – 10, how important is it for God to receive glory as a result of your life?

Day 3

Matthew 4:19 | Preparation

"Come, follow me," Jesus said, "and I will make you
fishers of men." (NIV)

Reflection Question: How did the previous careers of these
disciples prepare them for what Jesus would ask them to do? Are
there any parallels in your life since you started following Jesus?

Day 4

Philippians 2:12-13 | Shine On

Therefore, my dear friends, as you have always obeyed—not only in my
presence, but now much more in my absence—continue to work out your
salvation with fear and trembling, for it is God who works in you to will
and to act according to his good purpose. (NIV)

Reflection Question: Where would you like your relationship
with God to be a year from now? What's one step that
will move you in that direction?

Day 5

Philippians 1:6 | Extraordinary Work of Jesus

Being confident of this, that he who began a good work in you will carry it on to completion until the day of Christ Jesus. (NIV)

Reflection Question: In what ways do you recognize in your life right now the carrying on toward completion of Jesus work in you?

Weekly Memory Verse

Being confident of this, that he who began a good work in you will carry it on to completion until the day of Christ Jesus.
Philippians 1:6 (NIV)

SESSION 6

Be Extraordinary

If we

haven't learned anything else in these sessions, we've had a chance to see that there's nothing stereotypical about the details of an extraordinary life. God is infinitely creative (one of His largely ignored attributes), and He wants to practice that creativity in your life. You too can be extraordinary!

Angus Buchan

Farmers are a special breed. And Angus Buchan fits among them and has an amazing way of talking their language. But he's also a farmer who has learned over his lifetime that he is in the service and under the care of the Great Farmer and the Good Shepherd. He has come to see that the only almanac a farmer can really trust is called the Bible, God's Word. And he hasn't hesitated to put God's Word to the test, doing his best to be obedient to God's guidance and carrying out what God puts on his heart to do.

Angus Buchan set out in life to succeed as a farmer. And he's done it—twice. After being forced to leave a farm behind in one African country (Zimbabwe) because of civil war, he took his family and settled on raw land in South Africa and created a farm out of untamed land during a time of draught and difficulty. Angus wouldn't give up until he made it work. What he didn't expect was to discover that even when he wrestled the ground, the crops, and the cattle into submission, that he was deeply unsatisfied. Survival and even success didn't provide him with the kind of contentment and purpose he had hoped. In fact, Angus' moment of truth didn't come through disastrous failure; it came because success

failed. Angus reluctantly attended a lay witness gathering. he was introduced to Jesus and hasn't looked back since.

Most Biblical farmers and herders were driven men. They lived in the neighborhood of disaster at any moment. But whether they were very successful or miserable failures, every one of them had to learn (or they failed to learn) that the original curse in Eden, and life itself is never about succeeding without God. It's always about failing or succeeding with God.

Angus Buchan learned that lesson. His story is mostly about what God has been doing in his life since God harnessed all that drive for His own purposes. He has repeatedly taken God at His Word, doing things that were out of sync with common practice simply because he was following God's leading. Yes, he's had difficulties. The tragic and accidental death of a loved nephew under a tractor Angus was driving was a hard episode to experience, but God remained faithful.

Angus is still a farmer; but his fields are wider and longer, and farther away. And much of the seed he now plants is the seed of the Gospel in hearts that need to hear the good news about Jesus. Angus is living an extraordinary life!

COMING TOGETHER

In this final session of the series we are coming face to face with the choice we have been considering: what kind of life will we live. Daniel has been an excellent mentor to us over the last two sessions, showing us ways we can live for God in the midst of a hostile environment.

1 What would you say is one unforgettable idea that you are taking away from the last five sessions of *Your Extraordinary Life* that you believe will affect your life for a long time to come?

2 When you think of the word *extraordinary*, what events or persons would you use to illustrate the meaning for someone else? Why?

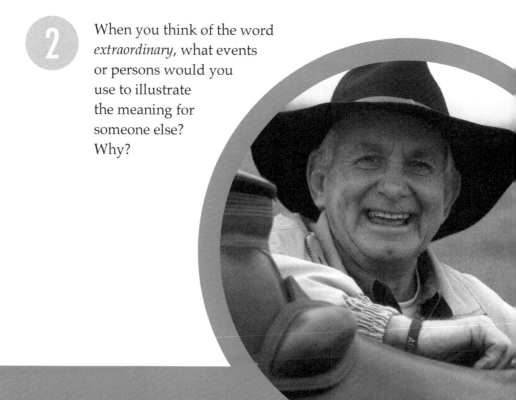

LEARNING TOGETHER

Throughout the sessions in *Your Extraordinary Life* we're hearing some pointed teaching from Pastor Allen Jackson as well as some personal stories from ordinary people who have lived extraordinary lives. We may not be led into quite the same life that Angus is leading but we can choose to live the extraordinary life God has designed for us. With that possibility in mind, let's begin our teaching for this session:

DVD SESSION 6

Use the space provided below for any notes, questions, or comments you want to bring up in the discussion later.

GROWING TOGETHER

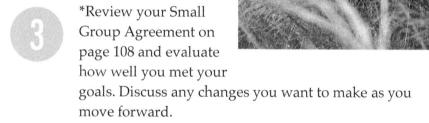

In the questions that follow, you will review and expand on the teaching you just experienced.

3 *Review your Small Group Agreement on page 108 and evaluate how well you met your goals. Discuss any changes you want to make as you move forward.

The video began with a definition of an extraordinary life: *A life with a purpose that transcends disappointments and injustice. A life that results in contentment, joy and fulfillment—both in time and eternity.* What do you find most challenging or exciting about this definition?

4 Romans 8:28 (NIV)
And we know that in all things God works for the good of those who love him, who have been called according to his purpose.

Describe a time God worked unexpectedly in a life circumstance for your good.

5

Galatians 5:7 (NIV)
You were running a good race. Who cut in on you and kept you from obeying the truth?

Can you remember an influence that caused you to lose God momentum in your life? Describe.

6

*You may not have ever heard Hebrews 12:2 used to describe Jesus as the writer of your life story, but in what ways do you recognize God has been involved in shaping your life?

7 *Two words were used to describe each of the three steps in God's outline for the story He's writing in our lives:

- Goal- Transformation/Relationship
- Difficulty- Singlemindedness/Preparation
- Requirements- Perseverance/Commitment

Pick any one of those six words and describe how you understand its importance in the life of faith?

8 How did each of the following Bible verses provide a key to living the extraordinary life?

And we know that in all things God works for the good of those who love him, who have been called according to his purpose. Romans 8:28

You were running a good race. Who cut in on you and kept you from obeying the truth? Galatians 5:7

Do you not know that in a race all the runners run, but only one gets the prize? Run in such a way as to get the prize. 1 Corinthians 9:24

GOING DEEPER

You can explore the following Bible passages behind the teaching for this session as a group (if there is time) or on your own between sessions.

Read Hebrews 12:1-13.
After a chapter filled with examples of faith, the writer of Hebrews turns the corner and asks us about how we're going to "run the race set before us."

How does this passage cover many of the themes we've touched on in *Your Extraordinary Life*?

Who are some the people whose opinions you value as you move along your spiritual journey?

What are some things you have had to set aside in order to continue growing in your faith?

Read 1 Corinthians 9:24 (NIV).

Do you not know that in a race all the runners run, but only one gets the prize? Run in such a way as to get the prize.

What attributes are required to win a race?

Is weariness an acceptable excuse for abandoning the race? Explain.

Describe a time when perseverance in your life or someone elses made a tremendous difference.

SHARING TOGETHER

9 How would you say your personal understanding and commitment to living an extraordinary life has been affected by this study?

10 What's one Scripture passage that you feel would most remind you of the various principles and insights covered in this study as you move toward a more extraordinary life?

GOING TOGETHER

During these sessions we are doing things "together:" learning, thinking, growing, praying, choosing, etc. Part of together is how we live when we aren't together.

 Take a few minutes to jot down three specific action steps that would move you further on the journey toward an extraordinary life.

      a. _____

      b. _____

      c. _____

 Now share at least one of these, if not all three, with the rest of the group to create a point of accountability, and give the group permission to ask you about your progress in this or these steps.

Close the session in prayer. Encourage each other to pray for others in the group.

DAILY REFLECTIONS

Day 1

John 10:10 | Abundant Living
The thief comes only to steal and kill and destroy; I have come that they may have life, and have it to the full. (NIV)

Reflection Question: What are some of the "thieves" you already know to watch out for as you pursue extraordinary living?

Day 2

Ephesians 2:10 | The Author
For we are God's workmanship, created in Christ Jesus to do good works, which God prepared in advance for us to do. (NIV)

Reflection Question: In what sense do you see your life as an example of God's extraordinary workmanship in Christ Jesus?

Day 3

Romans 8:28 | Extraordinary Circumstance

And we know that in all things God works for the good of those who love him, who have been called according to his purpose. (NIV)

Reflection Question: How does this verse encourage you as you pursue *Your Extraordinary Life*?

_____

_____

_____

_____

Day 4

1 Peter 2:21 | In His Steps

To this you were called, because Christ suffered for you, leaving you an example, that you should follow in his steps. (NIV)

Reflection Question: What examples of following in His steps might someone be able to identify in your life these days?

_____

_____

_____

_____

Day 5

Hebrews 12:1-2 | Steps to Extraordinary Life

Therefore, since we are surrounded by such a great cloud of witnesses, let us throw off everything that hinders and the sin that so easily entangles, and let us run with perseverance the race marked out for us. Let us fix our eyes on Jesus, the author and perfecter of our faith, who for the joy set before him endured the cross, scorning its shame, and sat down at the right hand of the throne of God. (NIV)

<u>Reflection Question:</u> In what areas of your life are you currently learning the importance of perseverance?

_____

_____

_____

_____

Weekly Memory Verse

And we know that in all things God works for the good of those who love him, who have been called according to his purpose. Romans 8:28 (NIV)

APPENDIX

Great resources to help
make your small group
experience even better!

FAQs

What do we do on the first night of our group?

Like all fun things in life–have a party! A "get to know you" coffee, dinner, or dessert is a great way to launch a new study. You may want to review the Group Agreement (page 108) and share the names of a few friends you can invite to join you. But most importantly, have fun before your study time begins.

Where do we find new members for our group?

We encourage you to pray with your group and then brainstorm a list of people from work, church, your neighborhood, your children's school, family, the gym, and so forth. Then have each group member invite several of the people on his or her list.

No matter how you find participants, it's vital that you stay on the lookout for new people to join your group. All groups tend to go through healthy attrition—the result of moves, releasing new leaders, ministry opportunities, and so forth—and if the group gets too small, it could be at risk of shutting down. If you and your group stay open, you'll be amazed at the people God sends your way. The next person just might become a friend for life. You never know!

How long will this group meet?

It's totally up to the group–once you come to the end of this 6-week study. Most groups meet weekly for at least their first 6 weeks, but every other week can work as well.

At the end of this study, each group member may decide if he or she wants to continue on for another 6-week study. Some groups launch relationships for years to come, and others are stepping-stones into another group experience. Either way, enjoy the journey.

Can we do this study on our own?

Absolutely! This may sound crazy but one of the best ways to do this study is not with a full house but with a few friends. You may choose to gather with one other couple who would enjoy going to the movies or having a quiet dinner and then walking through this study. Jesus will be with you even if there are only two of you (Matthew 18:20).

What if this group is not working for us?

You're not alone! This could be the result of a personality conflict, life stage difference, geographical distance, level of spiritual maturity, or any number of things. Relax. Pray for God's direction, and at the end of this 6-week study, decide whether to continue with this group or find another. You don't buy the first car you look at or marry the first person you date, and the same goes with a group. Don't bail out before the 6 weeks are up–God might have something to teach you. Also, don't run from conflict or prejudge people before you have given them a chance. God is still working in you too!

How do we handle the childcare needs in our group?

Very carefully. Seriously, this can be a sensitive issue. We suggest that you empower the group to openly brainstorm solutions. You may try one option that works for a while and then adjust over time. Our favorite approach is for adults to meet in the living room or dining room, and to share the cost of a babysitter (or two) who can be with the kids in a different part of the house. In this way, parents don't have to be away from their children all evening when their children are too young to be left at home. A second option is to use one home for the kids and a second home (close by or a phone call away) for the adults.

A third idea is to rotate the responsibility of providing a lesson or care for the children either in the same home or in another home nearby. This can be an incredible blessing for kids. Finally, the most common idea is to decide that you need to have a night to invest in your spiritual lives individually or as a couple, and to make your own arrangements for child care.

No matter what decision the group makes, the best approach is to dialogue openly about both the problem and the solution.

Small Group Agreement

Our Expectations:
To provide a predictable environment where participants experience authentic community and spiritual growth.

Group Attendance	To give priority to the group meeting. We will call or email if we will be late or absent. (Completing the Group Calendar will minimize this issue.)
Safe Environment	To help create a safe place where people can be heard and feel loved. (Please, no quick answers, snap judgments, or simple fixes.)
Respect Differences	To be gentle and gracious to people with different spiritual maturity, personal opinions, temperaments, or "imperfections" in fellow group members. We are all works in progress.
Confidentiality	To keep anything that is shared strictly confidential and within the group, and to avoid sharing improper information about those outside the group.
Encouragement for Growth	To be not just takers but givers of life. We want to spiritually multiply our life by serving others with our God-given gifts.
Shared Ownership	To remember that every member is a minister and to ensure that each attender will share a small responsibility over time.

Our Times Together:
- Refreshments/mealtimes _____
- Childcare _____
- When we will meet (day of week) _____
- Where we will meet (place) _____
- We will begin at (time) _____ and end at _____
- We will do our best to have some or all of us attend a worship service together.
  Our primary worship service time will be _____
- Date of this agreement _____
- Date we will review this agreement again _____
- Who (other than the leader) will review this agreement at the end of this study _____

Small Group Calendar

Planning and calendaring can help ensure the greatest participation at every meeting. At the end of each meeting, review this calendar. Don't forget birthdays, socials, church events, holidays, and mission/ministry projects.

Go to intendresources.com for an electronic copy of this form and more ideas for your group to do together.

Date	Lesson	Host Home	Dessert/Meal	Leader
11/16/2013	1	Steve and Laura's	Joe	Bill

Spiritual Partners' Checkin-In

Briefly check in each week and write down your personal plans and progress targets for the next week (or even for the next few weeks). This could be done (before or after the meeting) on the phone, through an e-mail message or even in person from time to time.

My Name:

Spiritual Partner's Name:

	Our Plan	Our Progress
Week 1		
Week 2		
Week 3		
Week 4		
Week 5		

Memory Verses

Session 1 — Genesis 1:31 (NIV)

God saw all that he had made, and it was very good. And there was evening, and there was morning--the sixth day.

Session 2 — Acts 17:27 (NIV)

God did this so that men would seek him and perhaps reach out for him and find him, though he is not far from each one of us.

Session 3 — Ephesians 4:15-16 (NIV)

Instead, speaking the truth in love, we will in all things grow up into him who is the Head, that is, Christ. From him the whole body, joined and held together by every supporting ligament, grows and builds itself up in love, as each part does its work.

Session 4 — Daniel 1:8 (NIV)

But Daniel resolved not to defile himself with the royal food and wine, and he asked the chief official for permission not to defile himself this way.

Session 5 — Philippians 1:6 (NIV)

Being confident of this, that he who began a good work in you will carry it on to completion until the day of Christ Jesus.

Session 6 — Romans 8:28 (NIV)

And we know that in all things God works for the good of those who love him, who have been called according to his purpose.

Prayer and Praise Report

	Prayer Requests	Priase Requests
Session 1	Mel- health /encouragement / family Judy- grandchildren to know lord Hec+Kathy - family /employers	
Session 2		
Session 3		
Session 4		
Session 5		
Session 6		

Small Group Roster

NAME	PHONE	EMAIL

SMALL GROUP LEADERS

Hosting an Open House

If you're starting a new group, try planning an "open house" before your first formal group meeting. Even if you only have two to four core members, it's a great way to break the ice and to consider prayerfully who else might be open to join you over the next few weeks. You can also use this kick-off meeting to hand out study guides, spend some time  getting to know each other, discuss each person's expectations for the group and briefly pray for each other.

A simple meal or good desserts always make a kick-off meeting more fun. After people introduce themselves and share how they ended up being at the meeting (you can play a game to see who has the wildest story!), have everyone respond to a few icebreaker questions: "What is your favorite family vacation?" or "What is one thing you love about your church/our community?" or "What are three things about your life growing up that most people here don't know?" Next, ask everyone to tell what he or she hopes to get out of the study. You might want to review the Small Group Agreement and talk about each person's expectations and priorities.

Finally, set an open chair (maybe two) in the center of your group and explain that it represents someone who would enjoy or benefit from this group but who isn't here yet. Ask people to pray about whom they could invite to join the group over the next few weeks. Hand out postcards and have everyone write an invitation or two. Don't worry about ending up with too many people; you can always have one discussion circle in the living room and another in the dining room after you watch the lesson. Each group could then report prayer requests and progress at the end of the session.

You can skip this kick-off meeting if your time is limited, but you'll experience a huge benefit if you take the time to connect with each other in this way.

Leading for the First Time

Sweaty palms are a healthy sign. The Bible says God is gracious to the humble. Remember who is in control; the time to worry is when you're not worried. Those who are soft in heart (and sweaty palmed) are those whom God is sure to speak through.

Seek support. Ask your leader, co-leader, or close friend to pray for you and prepare with you before the session. Walking through the study will help you anticipate potentially difficult questions and discussion topics.

Bring your uniqueness to the study. Lean into who you are and how God wants you to uniquely lead the study.

Prepare. Prepare. Prepare. Go through the session several times. If you are using the DVD, listen to the teaching segment and Leadership Lifter. Go to intendresources.com and download pertinent files. Consider writing in a journal or fasting for a day to prepare yourself for what God wants to do.

Ask for feedback so you can grow. Perhaps in an email or on cards handed out at the study, have everyone write down three things you did well and one thing you could improve on. Don't get defensive, but show an openness to learn and grow.

Use online resources. Go to intendresources.com and download additional notes or ideas for your session.

Prayerfully consider launching a new group. This doesn't need to happen overnight, but God's heart is for this to happen over time. Not all Christians are called to be leaders or teachers, but we are all called to be "shepherds" of a few someday.

Share with your group what God is doing in your heart. God is searching for those whose hearts are fully his. Share your trials and victories. We promise that people will relate.

Prayerfully consider whom you would like to pass the baton to next week. It's only fair. God is ready for the next member of your group to go on the faith journey you just traveled. Make it fun, and expect God to do the rest.

Leadership Training 101

Congratulations! You have responded to the call to help shepherd Jesus' flock. There are a few other tasks in the family of God that surpass the contribution you will be making. As you prepare to lead, whether it is one session or the entire series, here are a few thoughts to keep in mind. We encourage you to read these and review them with each new discussion leader before he or she leads.

1. Remember that you are not alone. God knows everything about you, and He knew that you would be asked to lead your group. Remember that it is common for all good leaders to feel that they are not ready to lead. Moses, Solomon, Jeremiah and Timothy—they all were reluctant to lead. God promises, *"Never will I leave you; never will I forsake you"* (Hebrews 13:5). Whether you are leading for one evening, for several weeks, or for a lifetime, you will be blessed as you serve.

2. Don't try to do it alone. Pray right now for God to help you build a healthy leadership team. If you can enlist a co-leader to help you lead the group, you will find your experience to be much richer. This is your chance to involve as many people as you can in building a healthy group. All you have to do is call and ask people to help, you'll be surprised at the response.

3. Just be yourself. If you won't be you, who will? God wants you to use your unique gifts and temperament. Don't try to do things exactly like another leader; do them in a way that fits you! Just admit it when you don't have an answer, and apologize when you make a mistake. Your group will love you for it, and you'll sleep better at night!

4. Prepare for your meeting ahead of time. Review the session and the leader's notes, and write down your responses to each question. Pay special attention to exercises that ask group members to do something other than engage in discussion. These exercises will help your group live what the Bible teaches, not just talk about it. Be sure you understand how an exercise works, and bring any necessary supplies (such as paper and pens) to your meeting. If the exercise employs one of the items in the appendix, be sure to look over that item so you'll know how it works. Finally, review "Outline for Each Session" so you'll remember the purpose of each section in the study.

5. Pray for your group members by name. Before you begin your session, go around the room in your mind and pray for each member by name. You may want to review the prayer list at least once a week. Ask God to use your time together to touch the heart of every person uniquely. Expect God to lead you to whomever He wants you to encourage or challenge in a special way. If you listen, God will surely lead!

6. When you ask a question, be patient. Someone will eventually respond. Sometimes people need a moment or two of silence to think about the question, and if silence doesn't bother you, it won't bother anyone else. After someone responds, affirm the response with a simple "thanks" or "good job." Then ask, "How about somebody else?" or "Would someone who hasn't shared like to add anything?" Be sensitive to new people or reluctant members who aren't ready to say, pray or do anything. If you give them a safe setting, they will blossom over time.

7. Provide transitions between questions. When guiding the discussion, always read aloud the transitional paragraphs and the questions. Ask the group if anyone would like to read the paragraph or Bible passage. Don't call on anyone, but ask for a volunteer, and then be patient until someone begins. Be sure to thank the person who reads aloud.

8. Break up into small groups each week, or they won't stay. If your group has more than seven people, we strongly encourage you to have the group gather sometimes in discussion circles of three or four people during the SHARING TOGETHER or GOING TOGETHER sections of the study. With a greater opportunity to talk in a small circle, people will connect more with the study, apply more quickly what they're learning and ultimately get more out of it. A small circle also encourages a quiet person to participate and tends to minimize the effects of a more vocal or dominant member. It can also help people feel more loved in your group. When you gather again at the end of the section, you can have one person summarize the highlights from each circle. Small circles are also helpful during prayer time. People who are unaccustomed to praying aloud will feel more comfortable trying it with just two or three others. Also, prayer requests won't take as much time, so circles will have more time to actually pray. When you gather back with the whole group, you can have one person from each circle briefly update everyone on the prayer requests. People are more willing to pray in small circles if they know that the whole group will hear all the prayer requests.

9. One final challenge (for new or first time leaders):
Before your first opportunity to lead, read each of the five passages listed below. Read each one as a devotional exercise to help equip yourself with a shepherd's heart. Trust us on this one. If you do this, you will be more than ready for your first meeting.

Matthew 9:36
1 Peter 5:2-4
Psalm 23
Ezekiel 34:11-16
1 Thessalonians 2:7-8, 11-12

G. Allen Jackson

G. Allen Jackson has worked with the congregation of World Outreach Church in Murfreesboro, Tennessee since 1981, serving as senior pastor for 22 years.

Under his leadership and vision, the World Outreach Church fellowship has grown from 150 to 10,000. In reaching the local community with the Gospel, the mission is clear—help people develop a meaningful relationship with God. Pastor Jackson spearheaded the development of a variety of World Outreach Church community events that provided opportunities for families to experience God, and for some, to become part of a local church. The results have been a stronger community, strengthened families and a healthier church.

Pastor Jackson earned a Bachelor of Arts from Oral Roberts University, a Master of Arts in Religious Studies from Vanderbilt University and studied at Hebrew University in Jerusalem. He has pursued additional studies at Gordon-Conwell Theological Seminary in Boston.

He is an active member of his community, having served on the Board of the American Red Cross and the Community Advisory Board of National Health Corporation Nursing Home. Pastor Jackson chaired the Murfreesboro Area Ministerial Association and was named Outstanding Young Minister by the Jr. Chamber of Commerce. He is a graduate of Leadership Rutherford, a community leadership program developed by the Chamber of Commerce. Jackson was honored as a distinguished community business leader by the Murfreesboro Chamber of Commerce in 2010.

Pastor Jackson has been a featured speaker at a conference conducted by the International Christian Embassy-Jerusalem Feast of Tabernacles celebration in Israel for several years. He has been recognized by the Christian Coalition of the Israeli Kennesset for his continued support. Pastor Jackson is a church planter and his passion is to help people, wherever they may be, to become fully devoted followers of Christ. His conviction in serving a God of restoration and effectuating a 24/7 church has touched people across the country and the world. Through Intend Ministries, Jackson coaches pastors across the nation and the world to greater effectiveness in their congregations.

Pastor Jackson is married, and his wife, Kathy, is an active participant in ministry at World Outreach Church.

FREEDOM FROM
WORRY
OVERCOMING ANXIETY
WITH GOD'S LOVE
PURPOSE
& POWER

WRITTEN BY
G. ALLEN JACKSON

Do not be anxious about anything, but in everything, by prayer and petition, with thanksgiving, present your requests to God. And the peace of God, which transcends all understanding, will guard your hearts and your minds in Christ Jesus.
Philippians 4:6-7

Worry contends with every one of us. To move beyond it is to press into life with a renewed vision of who God is, and with a recognition of His strength and provision in our lives. We need to know what God says about us, and we need to believe it.

"Sometimes the worries and anxieties of life can become so overwhelming we fear our world could suddenly collapse around us at any moment. We tend to look so close at our problems before us that they seem more than we could possibly handle... taking a step back we can see that God is bigger than the mountain. We need to have a new God prospective. This book will guide you through the steps to overcome worry and learn to live free in Christ. Praise God!"

Jane Leuthmers

Intend
G. Allen Jackson Faith Initiatives

1921 New Salem Road / HWY 99
Murfreesboro, TN 37128
(615) 896-4515 • intendresources.com

More from Intend Ministries

These and other resources available at intendresources.com

Your Extraordinary Life
SERMON CD/DVD SET

Order Pastor G. Allen Jackson's sermon series entitled "Your Extraordinary Life", available on both CD and DVD.

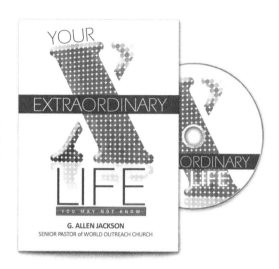

Your Extraordinary Life
PERSONAL JOURNAL

Have space for thoughts and prayers in this personal journal. Includes a 1-year chronological Bible reading plan.

INTEND MINISTRIES was launched to take the transforming message of God's Word to where people live—through radio and television broadcasts, web streaming, podcasting, books and other media tools. Helping people become more fully devoted followers of Jesus Christ is at the heart of Intend Ministries. Church leaders who want to make a difference and experience growth in their congregations are given practical tools for effectiveness, proven strategies for taking the "next step" in their ministry, and help in breaking the barriers of growth that every church faces. Intend Ministries has conducted seminars and training for church pastors and leaders, focusing on growth, leadership, creating and maintaining momentum, and vision casting.

Intend™

G. Allen Jackson Faith Initiatives

CPSIA information can be obtained at www.ICGtesting.com
Printed in the USA
LVOW010826210113

316523LV00003B/3/P